Jam Cookbook

Jam Making Cookbook with Homemade Jams and Jellies for Everyone

(Sunny Harvest in Jars)

Book 7

Brendan Fawn

Text Copyright © [Brendan Fawn]
All rights reserved. No part of this guide may be reproduced in any form without permission in writing from the publisher except in the case of brief quotations embodied in critical articles or reviews.

Legal & Disclaimer
The information contained in this book and its contents is not designed to replace or take the place of any form of medical or professional advice; and is not meant to replace the need for independent medical, financial, legal or other professional advice or services, as may be required. The content and information in this book has been provided for educational and entertainment purposes only.

The content and information contained in this book has been compiled from sources deemed reliable, and it is accurate to the best of the Author's knowledge, information and belief. However, the Author cannot guarantee its accuracy and validity and cannot be held liable for any errors and/or omissions. Further, changes are periodically made to this book as and when needed. Where appropriate and/or necessary, you must consult a professional (including but not limited to your doctor, attorney, financial advisor or such other professional advisor) before using any of the suggested remedies, techniques, or information in this book.

Upon using the contents and information contained in this book, you agree to hold harmless the Author from and against any damages, costs, and expenses, including any legal fees potentially resulting from the application of any of the information provided by this book. This disclaimer applies to any loss, damages or injury caused by the use and application, whether directly or indirectly, of any advice or information presented, whether for breach of contract, tort, negligence, personal injury, criminal intent, or under any other cause of action.

You agree to accept all risks of using the information presented in this book.

You agree that by continuing to read this book, where appropriate and/or necessary, you shall consult a professional (including but not limited to your doctor, attorney, or financial advisor or such other advisor as needed) before using any of the suggested remedies, techniques, or information in this book.

ISBN: 9798671708721

Introduction   6

Jams & Jellies – Sunny Desserts   7

Banana Taste Redcurrant Jam   10

Oranges Jelly   12

Sugar-Free Blueberry Jam   13

Homemade Strawberry Jam   14

Banana Strawberry Jam   16

Cashews Gooseberry Jam   18

Orange Cherry Jelly   20

Vanilla Strawberry Jam   21

Rose Petals & Cherry Jelly   23

Strawberry Jam   24

Melon & Orange Jelly   25

Lime-Strawberry Jam   26

Cherry-Redcurrant Jelly   28

Orange Raspberry Jam   29

Gooseberry and Raspberry Jam   30

Wild Cherry Jelly   31

Strawberry Peach Jam   32

Apples & Orange Jelly   33

Cherries & Plums Jelly 34

Pears-Alpine Strawberry Jam 35

Raspberry Jelly 37

Alpine Strawberry Orange Jam 38

Vanilla Blueberry Jelly 39

Orange Cherry Jam 40

Vanilla Cherry Jam 42

Apricots Taste Redcurrant Jelly 43

Redcurrant Jam 44

Plum and Blackcurrant Jelly 45

Apples & Blackcurrant Jam 47

Quince Jelly 48

Orange Quince Jam 49

Baked Orange Plum Jam 50

Orange Plum Jam 51

Baked Apple Jam 53

Vanilla Raspberry Jelly 54

Peach Jam 55

Pineapple Taste Cherry Jelly 57

Apricot Jam 58

Vanilla Apricot Jam 60

Sugar-Free Apricot Jam 62

Orange Apricot Jelly 64

Apple Pumpkin Jam 65

Orange Gooseberry Jam 66

Cherry Peach Jam 68

Lemon Apricot Jam 69

Vanilla Blueberry Jam 71

Vanilla Plum Jam 72

Baked Vanilla Plum Jam 74

Baked Pear Jam 76

Vanilla Apple Jam 78

Cherry Jelly with Raspberries and Oranges 79

Blueberry Pears Jelly 80

Mango-Raspberry Jam 81

Blackberry Jelly 82

Conclusion 83

Introduction

This cookbook contains sweet and colorful, homemade blueberry, plum raspberry, apricot and other jams, and jellies that could be prepared at home. I hope that every reader will find delicious and mouthwatering jams or jellies for himself and his family.

Housewives have their own secrets of how to cook tasty plum, peach, apricot, strawberry, orange or any other jam; however, there are common rules on how to prepare and preserve delicious jams long-term. In this jam cookbook, you will find these common directions and rules how to cook tasty jams and jellies in your home in your beloved kitchen.

What is more, you don't need to be a professional 28 Michelin Star chef to prepare delicious and tasty jams and jellies from this cookbook and to cook or bake tasty fruit desserts for yourself, your friends or family. I would like to encourage you to test these homemade jam recipes and to experiment with the ingredients adding your own sweet flavors!

Jams & Jellies – Sunny Desserts

Jam is a fruit or berry product, that is covered with sugar and then boiled or baked in a sugar syrup. Jam could be prepared from a variety of colorful and sweet fruits and berries - both traditional as pears, strawberries, cherries, raspberries, or apples, and exotic ones, for instance, kiwis, pineapples, bananas or mangos, as well as vegetables. For example, some fans of unusual vegetables and nuts jams prepare them from carrots, tomatoes, cucumbers, chestnuts, peanuts or walnuts. However, the most popular, without a doubt, are strawberry, raspberry, cherry, blackcurrant, blueberry, peach or apricot jams.

Homemade jam is one of the most delicious desserts. It could be used as a drug to treat a cold. I think there is no need to emphasize the benefits of raspberry, quince, cherry, blueberry, cranberry or any other jam. The presence of vital vitamins and microelements in jams and jellies makes them priceless. The most useful and healthy of course is jam, which is prepared in a so-called "cold" way without a heat. Fruits or berries are simply covered and ground with sugar.

Such jams contain the most nutrients and vitamins; however, these jams can be stored for a short period of time.

Tasty and fragrant colorful fruits jam, with the smell of the sun and heat, is especially pleasant to taste during the cold winter period, recalling the hot and sunny summer days. However, it is very important to choose the right fruits, berries or vegetables for jam or jelly. Ripe and fresh fruits of medium size are best suited to preserve the taste of natural berries and fruits, and what is more, when our jam is ready, to improve mood and give us a piece of summer during cold winter days. Fruit jam will give us energy and vitality as well because it has a lot of various vitamins, minerals, and trace elements.

Jams can have various colors and tastes and can be liquid and thick, sour, very sweet or with a hint of sweetness. We can cook them with the sugar or erythritol or choose natural "nature made" sweeteners such as honey or stevia. We should boil our jam over low or medium heat for around 30-50 minutes, stirring all the time and removing the scum and the foam from the jam surface.

This jam cookbook contains tasty homemade jams and jellies. Enjoy!

Banana Taste Redcurrant Jam

Prep Time: 40 min. | Makes around 5-6 10 oz jars

Ingredients:

30 oz redcurrants

5 cups of sugar

2 tbsp. lime juice

3 tsp. pure banana extract

How to Prepare:

1. In a large pot, boil the redcurrants over medium heat for about 40 minutes, stirring until the sugar dissolves. Skim the foam from the jam.

2. Ten minutes before the redcurrants jam is ready, mix in the lime juice and pure banana extract and keep stirring until the

redcurrants mixture has gelled enough. Continue boiling and testing every five minutes until the jam gets thick enough to ladle it into the jars.

3. Remove the saucepan with the redcurrants from the heat and ladle freshly cooked jam into the hot and sterilized jars up to 1/5 inch from the top.

4. Flip the jars with the redcurrants jam upside down or boil for around 10 minutes and then leave to cool. Check the lids by pressing them with the finger. In case some of the jars with the redcurrants jam are unsealed, place them into the fridge or reprocess the unsealed jars.

Nutritional Information (1 tbsp):
Calories: 48; Total fat: 4 oz; Total carbohydrates: 5 oz; Protein: 2 oz

Oranges Jelly

Prep Time: 1 hour | Makes: 8 10 oz jars

Ingredients:

3 lb oranges, peeled and diced

5 cups of sugar

2 tsp. vanilla

How to Prepare:

1. Spoon 1 cup of the sugar over the oranges. Set aside for overnight.
2. Boil the oranges over the low heat for around 30 minutes, stirring all the time. Pour in some water. Then mash the oranges using the potato masher and strain the mixture to get 4-5 cups of the juice.
3. In a saucepan, combine the juice with the remaining sugar and boil the juice for 30 minutes until thickened. The jelly should be thick enough to pour it into the jars. Skim the foam from the surface. 10 minutes before the jelly is ready mix in the vanilla.
4. Remove the saucepan from the heat and pour the freshly cooked jelly into the sterilized jars.
5. Turn the jars upside down or boil for around 10 minutes and then leave to cool. Check the lids by pressing them with the finger. In case some of the jars with the jelly are unsealed, place them into the fridge or reprocess the unsealed jars.

Nutritional Information (1 tbsp):

Calories: 57; Total fat: 4 oz; Total carbohydrates: 8 oz; Protein: 3 oz

Sugar-Free Blueberry Jam

Prep Time: 30 min. | Makes around 7 12 oz jars

Ingredients:

5 lb fresh blueberries, washed

4 tbsp. granulated erythritol

3 tbsp. stevia

2 tbsp. lemon juice

How to Prepare:

1. Boil the blueberries mixture with the erythritol over medium heat for around 30 minutes, stirring all the time until erythritol dissolves. Remove the foam from the jam surface while boiling. Keep stirring until the blueberries jam has gelled.

2. Add the stevia and lemon juice and remove the saucepan with the blueberries from the heat and pour the freshly cooked sugar-free blueberry jam into the sterilized jars up to 1/4 inch from the top and seal the jars.

3. Then turn the jars upside down and leave them for overnight to cool completely and only then turn them back or process in the water bath. Check the lids by pressing them with the finger. In case some of the jars with the sugar-free blueberries jam are unsealed, place them into the fridge or reprocess the unsealed jars.

Nutritional Information (1 tbsp):

Calories: 45; Total fat: 4 oz; Total carbohydrates: 8 oz; Protein: 3 oz

Homemade Strawberry Jam

Prep Time: 40 min. | Makes around 6 11 oz jars

Ingredients:

8 cups of strawberries

6 cups of sugar

2 tbsp. lemon juice, freshly squeezed

1 tsp. vanilla

How to Prepare:

1. Wash and then mash the strawberries with a potato masher, blender or food processor and then spoon the sugar over the crushed strawberries.

2. Boil the berries over medium heat for around 40 minutes, stirring all the time until the sugar dissolves and don't forget

to skim the foam from the strawberry jam. Add half cup of water and continue stirring.

3. 7-10 minutes before the strawberry jam is ready mix in the lemon juice and keep stirring until the strawberries mixture has thickened. Spoon some jam on a plate and wait until gelled, if not continue boiling and testing. When the jam is ready, remove the saucepan with the strawberries from the heat and spoon freshly cooked jam into sterilized jars up to 1/5 inch from the top.

4. Seal the jars and then turn them upside down. Leave the jars for overnight to cool completely and only then turn them back. Check the lids by pressing them with the finger. In case some of the jars are unsealed, place them into the fridge or reprocess the unsealed jars.

Nutritional Information (1 tbsp):

Calories: 68; Total fat: 0.1 oz; Total carbohydrates: 1 oz; Protcin: 1 oz

Banana Strawberry Jam

Prep Time: 40 min. | Makes around 7 10 oz jars

Ingredients:

5 lb small strawberries, washed

1 banana, chopped

4 cups of white sugar

0.5 oz pure banana extract

2 tsp. citric acid

2 tsp. vanilla

How to Prepare:

1. Place the strawberries and banana into a big saucepan and spoon the sugar over the fruits.

2. Boil the strawberries and banana mix over medium heat for around 40 minutes, stirring all the time until the sugar dissolves. Skim the foam from the surface.

3. Mix in the banana extract, citric acid, and vanilla and keep stirring until the strawberries mixture has gelled and thickened. Pour some jam on a plate and check if gelled, pressing it with the finger, if not continue boiling and testing.

4. Remove the saucepan with the strawberries and banana jam from the heat and pour freshly cooked jam into the hot jars up to 1/5 inch from the top.

5. Seal the jars and then turn them upside down. Leave the jars for overnight to cool completely and only then turn them back. Check the lids by pressing them with the finger. In case some of the jars are unsealed, place them into the fridge or reprocess the unsealed jars.

Nutritional Information (1 tbsp):

Calories: 63; Total fat: 4 oz; Total carbohydrates: 7 oz; Protein: 3 oz

Cashews Gooseberry Jam

Prep Time: 50 min. | *Makes: 7-8 10 oz jars*

Ingredients:

2 lb gooseberries

1 cup of cashews

4 cups of brown sugar

3 tbsp. lemon juice, squeezed

2 tsp. vanilla

How to Prepare:

1. Grind the cashews. In a bowl, combine the sugar with the vanilla and mix well.

2. Then place the gooseberries into a big saucepan and spoon the sugar-vanilla mixture on top and leave for at least 6 hours unrefrigerated at room temperature or place in the fridge overnight.

3. In the same saucepan boil the gooseberries and sugar-vanilla mixture over high heat for around 10 minutes, stirring all the time with a spoon until sugar dissolves.

4. Then reduce the heat and continue to boil for around 40 minutes but don't forget to skim the foam from the berries.

5. Pour the lemon juice and add the nuts. Keep stirring until the berries mixture has gelled and thickened.

6. Remove the saucepan with the gooseberries from the heat and pour the freshly cooked jam into the sterilized jars up to 1/5 inch from the top.

7. Seal the jars and then turn the jars upside down. Leave them for overnight to cool completely and only then turn them back.

Nutritional Information (1 tbsp):

Calories: 67; Total fat: 1 oz; Total carbohydrates: 4 oz; Protein: 0.8 oz

Orange Cherry Jelly

Prep Time: 1 hour | Makes: 6-7 11 oz jars

Ingredients:

2 lbs cherries, pitted

2 cups of orange juice

5 cups of sugar

2 tsp. citric acid

How to Prepare:

1. Spoon 1 cup of sugar over the berries and set aside for overnight.
2. Boil the berries over the low heat for around 30 minutes, stirring all the time. Then mash the berries with the potato masher and strain the mixture to get 4-5 cups of the juice.
3. In a saucepan, combine the juice with the remaining sugar and boil the juice for 30 minutes until thickened. Pour the orange juice. The jelly should be thick enough to pour it into the jars. Skim the foam from the surface. 10 minutes before the jelly is ready mix in the citric acid.
4. Remove the saucepan from the heat and pour the freshly cooked jelly into the sterilized jars.
5. Turn the jars upside down or boil for around 10 minutes and then leave to cool. Check the lids by pressing them with the finger. In case some of the jars with the cherry jelly are unsealed, place them into the fridge or reprocess the unsealed jars.

Nutritional Information (1 tbsp):

Calories: 57; Total fat: 4 oz; Total carbohydrates: 8 oz; Protein: 3 oz

Vanilla Strawberry Jam

Prep Time: 50 min. | *Makes: 7-8 10 oz jars*

Ingredients:

5 lb fresh strawberries

6 cups of sugar

2 tsp. cinnamon

How to Prepare:

1. Place the strawberries into a big saucepan and spoon the sugar on top. Then sprinkle the cinnamon and leave for at least 6 hours unrefrigerated at room temperature or place in the fridge overnight.
2. In the same saucepan boil the strawberries and sugar-vanilla mixture over high heat for around 10 minutes, stirring all the time with a spoon until sugar dissolves.
3. Then reduce the heat and continue to boil for around 40 minutes but don't forget to skim the foam from the strawberries.
4. Pour the lemon juice and keep stirring until the strawberries mixture has gelled and thickened.
5. Remove the saucepan with the strawberries from the heat and pour freshly cooked jam into sterilized jars up to 1/5 inch from the top.
6. Seal the jars and then turn the jars upside down. Leave them for overnight to cool completely and only then turn them back.
7. Or you can do it more traditionally by placing the jars into the water bath and boiling for around 7-10 minutes and then leaving to cool. Check the lids by pressing them with the finger. In case some of the jars with the vanilla and

strawberry jam are unsealed, place them into the fridge or reprocess the unsealed jars.

Nutritional Information (1 tbsp):

Calories: 69; Total fat: 2 oz; Total carbohydrates: 3 oz; Protein: 0.7 oz

Rose Petals & Cherry Jelly

Prep Time: 1 hour | Makes: 6-7 11 oz jars

Ingredients:

2 lbs cherries, pitted

2 cups of rose petals

5 cups of sugar

2 tsp. citric acid

How to Prepare:

1. Spoon 1 cup of the sugar over the berries and set aside for overnight. In a pan, heat the water and boil the rose petals on a low heat for about 15 minutes.

2. Boil the berries over the low heat for around 30 minutes, stirring all the time. Then mash the berries with the potato masher and strain the mixture to get 4-5 cups of the juice.

3. In a saucepan, combine the juice with the remaining sugar and rose petals. Boil the juice for 30 minutes until thickened. Pour the orange juice. The jelly should be thick enough to pour it into the jars. Skim the foam from the surface. 10 minutes before the jelly is ready mix in the citric acid.

4. Remove the saucepan from the heat and pour the freshly cooked jelly into the sterilized jars.

5. Turn the jars upside down or boil for around 10 minutes and then leave to cool. Check the lids by pressing them with the finger. In case some of the jars with the cherry jelly are unsealed, place them into the fridge or reprocess the unsealed jars.

Nutritional Information (1 tbsp):

Calories: 57; Total fat: 4 oz; Total carbohydrates: 8 oz; Protein: 3 oz

Strawberry Jam

Prep Time: 35 min. | Makes: 7-8 12 oz jars

Ingredients:

5 lb fresh strawberries, halved

6.5 cups of sugar

3 tbsp. lemon juice, freshly squeezed

1 tsp. cinnamon

How to Prepare:

1. In a saucepan, combine the sugar and 1.5 cup of water and bring the mixture to the boil.

2. Add the strawberries and boil over medium heat for around 30 minutes, stirring all the time with a spoon until the sugar dissolves and don't forget to skim the foam from the strawberry jam.

3. 5 min. before the jam is ready mix in the lemon juice and cinnamon and keep stirring until the strawberries mixture has thickened and gelled. Spoon some jam on a plate and wait until thickened, if not continue boiling and testing every 5 minutes.

4. Remove the saucepan with the strawberries from the heat and spoon freshly cooked jam into sterilized jars up to 1/5 inch from the top.

5. Seal the jars and then turn the jars upside down. Leave them for overnight to cool completely and only then turn them back. Check the lids by pressing them with the finger. In case some of the jars with the strawberry jam are unsealed, place them into the fridge or reprocess the unsealed jars.

Nutritional Information (1 tbsp):
Calories: 90; Total fat: 0.2 oz; Total carbohydrates: 4 oz; Protein: 0.1 oz

Melon & Orange Jelly

Prep Time: 1 hour | Makes: 8 10 oz jars

Ingredients:

2 lb oranges, peeled and diced

1 medium melon (20 oz), peeled and diced

5 cups of sugar

2 tsp. pure vanilla extract

How to Prepare:

1. Spoon 1 cup of the sugar over the oranges. Set aside for overnight.
2. Boil the oranges over the low heat for around 30 minutes, stirring all the time. Pour in some water. Then mash the oranges the potato masher and strain the mixture to get 4-5 cups of the juice.
3. In a saucepan, combine the juice with the remaining sugar and melon. Boil the juice for 30 minutes until thickened. The jelly should be thick enough to pour it into the jars. Skim the foam from the surface. 10 minutes before the jelly is ready mix in the vanilla.
4. Remove the saucepan from the heat and pour the freshly cooked jelly into the sterilized jars.
5. Turn the jars upside down or boil for around 10 minutes and then leave to cool. Check the lids by pressing them with the finger. In case some of the jars with the jelly are unsealed, place them into the fridge or reprocess the unsealed jars.

Nutritional Information (1 tbsp):

Calories: 54; Total fat: 4 oz; Total carbohydrates: 7 oz; Protein: 3 oz

Lime-Strawberry Jam

Prep Time: 50 min. | Makes: 9-10 8 oz jars

Ingredients:

4 lb fresh and sweet strawberries

5 limes, peeled and diced

4 cups of sugar

1 tsp. vanilla

How to Prepare:

1. Spoon 2 cups of the sugar over the diced limes. Leave for at least 3 hours unrefrigerated at room temperature or place in the fridge overnight. Place the strawberries into a big saucepan and boil with the remaining sugar and limes.
2. Boil the strawberries mixture over medium heat for around 30 minutes, stirring all the time until the sugar dissolves.

Remove the foam from the strawberries jam while boiling. Keep stirring until the strawberries jam has gelled.

3. Remove the saucepan with the strawberries from the heat and pour freshly cooked jam into sterilized jars up to 1/5 inch from the top.

4. Seal the jars and then turn the jars upside down. Leave them for overnight to cool completely and only then turn them back. Check the lids by pressing them with the finger. In case some of the jars with the strawberry jam are unsealed, place them into the fridge or reprocess the unsealed jars.

Nutritional Information (1 tbsp):

Calories: 50; Total fat: 4 oz; Total carbohydrates: 3 oz; Protein: 2 oz

Cherry-Redcurrant Jelly

Prep Time: 50 min. | Makes: 6-7 11 oz jars

Ingredients:

6 cups of redcurrants, fresh

2 cups of sweet cherry syrup

5 cups of sugar

1 tbsp. pure vanilla extract

How to Prepare:

1. Spoon 4 tbsp. sugar over the redcurrants and set aside for few hours and then mash the berries with the potato masher.
2. Pour some water and boil the redcurrants over the low heat for around 15-20 minutes, stirring all the time. Then strain the redcurrants to get 4 cups of the juice.
3. In a saucepan, combine the juice with the cherry syrup and sugar and boil the juice for 30 minutes. The jelly should be thick enough to ladle it into the jars. If not, add more sugar. Remove the foam from the surface.
4. Remove the saucepan from the heat and ladle the freshly cooked jelly into the sterilized jars and seal the jars.
5. Flip the jars upside down or boil for around 10 minutes and then leave to cool. Check the lids by pressing them with the finger. In case some of the jars with the redcurrant jelly are unsealed, place them into the fridge or reprocess the unsealed jars.

Nutritional Information (1 tbsp):

Calories: 54; Total fat: 2 oz; Total carbohydrates: 9 oz; Protein: 3 oz

Orange Raspberry Jam

Prep Time: 40 min. | Makes: 5-6 11 oz jars

Ingredients:

3 lb fresh and sweet raspberries

2 tbsp. orange zest, minced

5 cups of sugar

3 tbsp. orange juice, freshly squeezed

How to Prepare:
1. Spoon the raspberries into a food processor or blender and lightly puree them to have halves of the berries.
2. In a large saucepan, combine the raspberries and sugar and boil over medium heat for around 40 minutes, stirring all the time with a spoon until the sugar dissolves. Take a big spoon and skim the foam from the raspberry jam.
3. Spoon some jam on a plate and wait until thickened, if not continue boiling and testing. The jam should be thick enough to spoon it into jars. Few minutes before the jam is ready stir in the orange juice and orange zest and keep stirring until the raspberries mixture has thickened.
4. When the jam is ready, remove the saucepan with the raspberries from the heat and spoon freshly cooked jam into sterilized jars up to 1/5 inch from the top.
5. Seal the jars and then process them in a water bath. In a large pot, boil the jars for around 10 minutes and then take them out and leave to cool. Check the lids by pressing them with the finger. In case some of the jars with the raspberry jam are unsealed, place them into the fridge or reprocess the unsealed jars.

Nutritional Information (1 tbsp):
Calories: 72; Total fat: 0.2 oz; Total carbohydrates: 2.8 oz; Protein: 0 oz

Gooseberry and Raspberry Jam

Prep Time: 40 min. | *Makes: 5-6 11 oz jars*

Ingredients:

1.5 lb gooseberries

1.5 lb raspberries

5 cups of sugar

1 tbsp. lemon juice or half tsp. citric acid

How to Prepare:

1. In a big pot, combine berries with the sugar and leave for 2 hours unrefrigerated at room temperature.

2. Boil the berries with the sugar for 40 minutes, stirring until the sugar dissolves and removing the foam and scum from the surface.

3. 5 minutes before the jam is ready mix in the lemon juice or citric acid and keep stirring until the berries jam has thickened.

4. Ladle freshly cooked berries jam into sterilized jars up to 1/4 inch from the top and then seal the jars.

5. Now turn the jars upside down and leave them for at least 5 hours or for overnight to cool completely and only then turn them back. Check the lids by pressing them with the finger. In case some of the jars with the gooseberry jam are unsealed, place them into the fridge or reprocess the unsealed jars.

Nutritional Information (1 tbsp):

Calories: 64; Total fat: 3 oz; Total carbohydrates: 7 oz; Protein: 4 oz

Wild Cherry Jelly

Prep Time: 1 hour | Makes: 8-10 10 oz jars

Ingredients:

4 lbs wild cherries, pitted

5 cups of sugar

2 tsp. citric acid

How to Prepare:

1. Spoon 1 cup of sugar over the berries and set aside for overnight.
2. Pour some water and boil the berries over the low heat for around 30 minutes, stirring all the time. Then mash the berries with the potato masher and strain the mixture to get 4-5 cups of the juice.
3. In a saucepan, combine the juice with the remaining sugar and boil the juice for 30 minutes until thickened. The jelly should be thick enough to pour it into the jars. Skim the foam from the surface. 10 minutes before the jelly is ready mix in the citric acid.
4. Remove the saucepan from the heat and pour the freshly cooked jelly into the sterilized jars.
5. Turn the jars upside down or boil for around 10 minutes and then leave to cool. Check the lids by pressing them with the finger. In case some of the jars with the wild cherry jelly are unsealed, place them into the fridge or reprocess the unsealed jars.

Nutritional Information (1 tbsp):

Calories: 57; Total fat: 4 oz; Total carbohydrates: 8 oz; Protein: 3 oz

Strawberry Peach Jam

Prep Time: 40 min. | *Makes: 5-6 11 oz jars*

Ingredients:

2.5 lb peaches, washed and sliced

2 lb small strawberries

5 cups of sugar

1 tbsp. lemon juice or 1 tsp. citric acid

How to Prepare:

1. In a big pot, combine the sliced peaches with the strawberries and add the sugar on top. Leave for 5 hours unrefrigerated at room temperature.

2. Boil the fruits with the sugar for 40 minutes, stirring until the sugar dissolves. Take a big spoon and remove the foam from the jam surface.

3. 5 minutes before the jam is ready mix in the lemon juice or citric acid and keep stirring until the jam has thickened.

4. Spoon the freshly cooked peach jam into sterilized jars up to 1/5 inch from the top and then seal the jars.

5. Now turn the jars upside down and leave them for at least 5 hours or for overnight to cool completely and only then turn them back. Check the lids by pressing them with the finger. In case some of the jars with the strawberry peach jam are unsealed, place them into the fridge or reprocess the unsealed jars.

Nutritional Information (1 tbsp):

Calories: 70; Total fat: 3 oz; Total carbohydrates: 8 oz; Protein: 5 oz

Apples & Orange Jelly

Prep Time: 1 hour | Makes: 8 10 oz jars

Ingredients:

2 lb apples, diced

4 oranges, peeled and diced

5 cups of sugar

2 tsp. cinnamon

How to Prepare:

1. Spoon 1 cup of the sugar over the apples and oranges. Set aside for overnight.
2. Boil the apples and oranges over the low heat for around 30 minutes, stirring all the time. Pour in some water. Then mash the apples and oranges using the potato masher and strain the mixture to get 4-5 cups of the juice.
3. In a saucepan, combine the juice with the remaining sugar and boil the juice for 30 minutes until thickened. The jelly should be thick enough to pour it into the jars. Skim the foam from the surface. 10 minutes before the jelly is ready mix in the cinnamon.
4. Remove the saucepan from the heat and pour the freshly cooked jelly into the sterilized jars.
5. Turn the jars upside down or boil for around 10 minutes and then leave to cool. Check the lids by pressing them with the finger. In case some of the jars with the jelly are unsealed, place them into the fridge or reprocess the unsealed jars.

Nutritional Information (1 tbsp):

Calories: 57; Total fat: 4 oz; Total carbohydrates: 8 oz; Protein: 3 oz

Cherries & Plums Jelly

Prep Time: 1 hour | Makes: 6-7 11 oz jars

Ingredients:

2 lbs cherries, pitted

1 lbs plums, pitted

5 cups of sugar

2 tsp. citric acid

How to Prepare:

1. Spoon 1 cup of sugar over the berries and set aside for overnight.

2. Pour some water and boil the berries with the over low heat for around 30 minutes, stirring all the time. Then mash the berries with the potato masher and strain the mixture to get 4-5 cups of the juice.

3. In a saucepan, combine the juice with the remaining sugar and boil the juice for 30 minutes until thickened. The jelly should be thick enough to pour it into the jars. Skim the foam from the surface. 10 minutes before the jelly is ready mix in the citric acid.

4. Remove the saucepan from the heat and pour the freshly cooked jelly into the sterilized jars.

5. Turn the jars upside down or boil for around 10 minutes and then leave to cool. Check the lids by pressing them with the finger. In case some of the jars with the cherry jelly are unsealed, place them into the fridge or reprocess the unsealed jars.

Nutritional Information (1 tbsp):

Calories: 65; Total fat: 5 oz; Total carbohydrates: 7 oz; Protein: 3 oz

Pears-Alpine Strawberry Jam

Prep Time: 40 min. | Makes: 3-4 10 oz jars

Ingredients:

2-2.5 lb Alpine strawberries

4 medium pears, diced

4 cups of sugar

1 tsp. citric acid

How to Prepare:

1. Spoon the sugar over the Alpine strawberries and pears. Set aside for at least few hours.

2. Boil the Alpine strawberries with the pears and sugar over medium heat for 40 minutes, stirring all the time until thickened. Remove the scum from the surface. Few minutes before the jam is ready mix in the citric acid.

3. Pour the Alpine strawberries and pears jam into the sterilized jars up to 1/5 inch from the top.

4. Seal the jars and then flip the jars upside down or boil for around 7-10 minutes and then leave to cool. Check the lids by pressing them with the finger. In case some of the jars with the Alpine strawberry jam are unsealed, place them into the fridge or reprocess the unsealed jars.

Nutritional Information (1 tbsp):

Calories: 70; Total fat: 2 oz; Total carbohydrates: 8 oz; Protein: 3 oz

Raspberry Jelly

Prep Time: 50 min. | Makes: 7-8 10 oz jars

Ingredients:

25 oz raspberries, fresh

5 cups of sugar

1 medium lemon, halved and squeezed

3 tbsp. pure vanilla extract

How to Prepare:

1. Spoon 4 tbsp. sugar over the raspberries. Set aside for few hours. Then mash the raspberries using the potato masher.
2. Pour some water and boil the raspberries on a low heat for around 15-20 minutes, stirring all the time. Then strain the raspberries to get 4 cups of the juice.
3. In a saucepan, combine the juice with the sugar and pure vanilla extract. Pour the lemon juice. Boil the strawberry juice for 30 minutes. The jelly should be thick enough to pour it into the jars.
4. Remove the saucepan from the heat and ladle the freshly cooked jelly into the sterilized jars and seal the jars.
5. Flip the jars upside down or boil for around 10 minutes and then leave to cool. Check the lids by pressing them with the finger. In case some of the jars with the raspberry jelly are unsealed, place them into the fridge or reprocess the unsealed jars.

Nutritional Information (1 tbsp):

Calories: 52; Total fat: 3 oz; Total carbohydrates: 8 oz; Protein: 2 oz

Alpine Strawberry Orange Jam

Prep Time: 40 min. | Makes: 3-4 10 oz jars

Ingredients:

2-2.5 lb Alpine strawberries

1 tbsp. orange zest, minced

4 cups of sugar

1 tbsp. orange juice

How to Prepare:

1. Spoon the sugar over the Alpine strawberries and set aside for at least few hours.

2. Boil the Alpine strawberries with the sugar over medium heat for 40 minutes, stirring all the time until thickened. Remove the scum from the surface. Few minutes before the jam is ready mix in the orange zest and orange juice.

3. Pour the Alpine strawberry jam into sterilized jars up to 1/4 inch from the top and seal the jars. Then flip the jars upside down or boil for around 10 minutes and then leave to cool. Check the lids by pressing them with the finger. In case some of the jars with the Alpine strawberry orange jam are unsealed, place them into the fridge or reprocess the unsealed jars.

Nutritional Information (1 tbsp):

Calories: 53; Total fat: 2 oz; Total carbohydrates: 7 oz; Protein: 3 oz

Vanilla Blueberry Jelly

Prep Time: 1 hour | Makes: 6-7 11 oz jars

Ingredients:

3 lbs blueberries

5 cups of sugar

2 tsp. citric acid

2 tsp. vanilla

How to Prepare:

1. Spoon 1 cup of the sugar over the berries and set aside for overnight.
2. Boil the blueberries over the low heat for around 30 minutes, stirring all the time. Pour in some water. Then mash the blueberries with the potato masher and strain the mixture to get 4-5 cups of the juice.
3. In a saucepan, combine the juice with the remaining sugar and vanilla and boil the juice for 30 minutes until thickened. The jelly should be thick enough to pour it into the jars. Skim the foam from the surface. 10 minutes before the jelly is ready mix in the citric acid.
4. Remove the saucepan from the heat and pour the freshly cooked jelly into the sterilized jars.
5. Turn the jars upside down or boil for around 10 minutes and then leave to cool. Check the lids by pressing them with the finger. In case some of the jars with the jelly are unsealed, place them into the fridge or reprocess the unsealed jars.

Nutritional Information (1 tbsp):

Calories: 57; Total fat: 4 oz; Total carbohydrates: 8 oz; Protein: 3 oz

Orange Cherry Jam

Prep Time: 20 min. | Makes: 4-5 11 oz jars

Ingredients:

4 cups of cherries, washed and pitted

3 tbsp. orange zest, minced

4 cups of sugar

3 tbsp. orange juice

How to Prepare:

1. Spoon the sugar over the cherries and pour few glasses of water, and then boil the cherries over low heat for 15-20 minutes, stirring all the time.

2. Remove the foam from the surface and stir in the orange zest and orange juice.

3. Remove the saucepan from the heat and ladle the freshly cooked jam into the sterilized jars and seal them.

4. Flip the jars upside down or boil for around 10 minutes and then leave to cool. Check the lids by pressing them with the finger. In case some of the jars are unsealed, place them into the fridge or reprocess the unsealed jars.

Nutritional Information (1 tbsp):

Calories: 57; Total fat: 5 oz; Total carbohydrates: 8 oz; Protein: 2 oz

Vanilla Cherry Jam

Prep Time: 20 min. | Makes: 4-5 11 oz jars

Ingredients:

4 cups of cherries, washed and pitted

1 tbsp. vanilla

4 cups of sugar

1 tsp. citric acid

How to Prepare:

1. Spoon the sugar over the cherries and pour few glasses of water, and then boil the cherries over low heat for 15-20 minutes, stirring all the time.
2. Remove the foam from the surface and stir in the vanilla.
3. Remove the saucepan from the heat and ladle the freshly cooked jam into the sterilized jars and seal them.
4. Flip the jars upside down or boil for around 10 minutes and then leave to cool. Check the lids by pressing them with the finger. In case some of the jars with the cherry jam are unsealed, place them into the fridge or reprocess the unsealed jars.

Nutritional Information (1 tbsp):

Calories: 55; Total fat: 1 oz; Total carbohydrates: 3 oz; Protein: 1.5 oz

Apricots Taste Redcurrant Jelly

Prep Time: 50 min. | Makes: 6-7 11 oz jars

Ingredients:

6 cups of redcurrants, fresh

3 tbsp. pure apricots extract

5 cups of sugar

1 cup of orange juice

How to Prepare:

1. Spoon 4 tbsp. sugar over the redcurrants and set aside for few hours and then crush the berries.

2. Pour some water and boil the redcurrants over the low heat for 15-20 minutes, stirring all the time. Then strain the redcurrants to get 4 cups of the juice.

3. In a saucepan, combine the juice with the sugar and boil the juice for 30 minutes. Pour the orange juice. Mix well. The jelly should be thick enough to ladle it into the jars. Remove the foam from the surface. 10 minutes before the jelly is ready mix in the pure apricots extract.

4. Remove the saucepan from the heat and ladle the freshly cooked jelly into the sterilized jars and seal the jars.

5. Flip the jars upside down or boil for around 10 minutes and then leave to cool. Check the lids by pressing them with the finger. In case some of the jars with the redcurrant jelly are unsealed, place them into the fridge or reprocess the unsealed jars.

Nutritional Information (1 tbsp):

Calories: 56; Total fat: 3 oz; Total carbohydrates: 5 oz; Protein: 3 oz

Redcurrant Jam

Prep Time: 40 min. | Makes: 5-6 11 oz jars

Ingredients:

4 cups of redcurrants, fresh

6 cups of sugar

1 tsp. vanilla

How to Prepare:

1. Wash the redcurrants and boil the berries with the sugar over medium heat for 40 minutes, stirring all the time until thickened. Remove the foam from the surface.

2. Spoon some jam on a plate and wait until thickened, if not continue boiling and testing. The jam should be thick enough to spoon it into jars. Few minutes before the jam is ready stir in the vanilla.

3. When the jam is ready, remove the saucepan from the heat and ladle freshly cooked redcurrant jam into sterilized jars up to 1/5 inch from the top and seal the jars.

4. Flip the jars with the redcurrant jam upside down or boil for around 10 minutes and then leave to cool. Check the lids by pressing them with the finger. In case some of the jars with the redcurrant jam are unsealed, place them into the fridge or reprocess the unsealed jars.

Nutritional Information (1 tbsp):

Calories: 54; Total fat: 5 oz; Total carbohydrates: 8 oz; Protein: 2 oz

Plum and Blackcurrant Jelly

Prep Time: 50 min. | Makes: 6-7 11 oz jars

Ingredients:

6 cups of blackcurrants, fresh

1 lbs plums, pitted

4 cups of sugar

1 tsp. citric acid

1 tsp. vanilla

How to Prepare:

1. Spoon 4 tbsp. sugar over the blackcurrants and plums. Set aside for few hours and then mash the berries using the potatoes masher.
2. Pour some water and boil the blackcurrants and plums over low heat for 15-20 minutes, stirring all the time. Then strain the blackcurrants and plums to get 4-5 cups of the juice.

3. In a saucepan, combine the juice with the sugar and vanilla and boil the juice for 30 minutes. The jelly should be thick enough to ladle it into the jars. Remove the foam from the surface.

4. Remove the saucepan from the heat and ladle the freshly cooked jelly into the sterilized jars and seal the jars.

5. Flip the jars upside down or boil for around 10 minutes and then leave to cool. In case some of the jars with the blackcurrant jelly are unsealed, place them into the fridge or reprocess the unsealed jars.

Nutritional Information (1 tbsp):

Calories: 57; Total fat: 4 oz; Total carbohydrates: 5 oz; Protein: 3 oz

Apples & Blackcurrant Jam

Prep Time: 40 min. | Makes: 6-7 11 oz jars

Ingredients:

2.5 lbs blackcurrants

2 lbs apples, peeled and diced

5 cups of sugar

2 tbsp. orange juice

How to Prepare:

1. Boil the blackcurrants with the apples and sugar over medium heat for around 40 minutes, stirring all the time and removing the foam from the surface.

2. Spoon some jam on a plate and wait until thickened, if not continue boiling and testing until gelled. The jam should be thick enough to ladle it into the jars. 10 minutes before the jam is ready mix in the orange zest and orange juice.

3. Remove the saucepan from the heat and ladle freshly cooked jam into sterilized jars up to 1/5 inch from the top and seal the jars.

4. Flip the jars with the jam upside down or boil for around 10 minutes and then leave to cool. In case some of the jars with the blackcurrant jam are unsealed, place them into the fridge or reprocess the unsealed jars.

Nutritional Information (1 tbsp):

Calories: 53; Total fat: 4 oz; Total carbohydrates: 8 oz; Protein: 3 oz

Quince Jelly

Prep Time: 1 hour | Makes: 6-7 11 oz jars

Ingredients:

8 cups of quinces, halved

6 cups of sugar

1 tsp. citric acid

1 tsp. cinnamon

How to Prepare:

1. Slice the quinces and spoon 1 cup of sugar over them and set aside for overnight.
2. Heat 5 cups of water and boil the quinces over medium heat for 30 minutes, stirring all the time. Then strain the quince mixture to get 4-5 cups of the juice.
3. In a saucepan, combine the juice with the remaining sugar and boil the juice for 30 minutes until thickened. The jelly should be thick enough to pour it into the jars. Skim the foam from the surface. 10 minutes before the jelly is ready mix in the citric acid.
4. Remove the saucepan from the heat and pour the freshly cooked jelly into the sterilized jars.
5. Turn the jars upside down or boil for around 10 minutes and then leave to cool. Check the lids by pressing them with the finger. In case some of the jars with the quince jelly are unsealed, place them into the fridge or reprocess the unsealed jars.

Nutritional Information (1 tbsp):

Calories: 49; Total fat: 4 oz; Total carbohydrates: 5 oz; Protein: 3 oz

Orange Quince Jam

Prep Time: 50 min. | Makes: 6-7 11 oz jars

Ingredients:

8 cups of quinces, halved

6 cups of sugar

1 tbsp. orange zest, minced

4 tbsp. orange juice

1 tsp. vanilla

How to Prepare:

1. Process the quinces in a food processor or blender and boil with the sugar and few cups of water over medium heat for around 50 minutes, stirring all the time until gelled. Remove the foam from the surface.

2. Spoon some jam on a plate and wait until thickened and gelled, if not continue boiling and testing. The jam should be thick enough to spoon it into the jars. 5 minutes before the jam is ready stir in the orange zest and orange juice.

3. When the quince jam is ready, remove the saucepan from the heat and ladle freshly cooked jam into sterilized jars up to 1/5 inch from the top to seal the jars.

4. Then process the jars with the jam in a water bath. In a large pot, boil the jars for around 10 minutes and then take them out and leave to cool. Check the lids by pressing them with the finger. In case some of the jars with the quince jam are unsealed, place them into the fridge or reprocess the unsealed jars.

Nutritional Information (1 tbsp):

Calories: 57; Total fat: 4 oz; Total carbohydrates: 2.1 oz; Protein: 2 oz

Baked Orange Plum Jam

Prep Time: 2 hours | Makes: 6-7 11 oz jars

Ingredients:

5 lb plums, pitted and halved

2 tbsp. orange zest, minced

4 cups of sugar

2 tbsp. orange juice

1 tsp. cinnamon

How to Prepare:

1. Combine the plums with the sugar and preheat the oven to 300°-360° Fahrenheit. Mix in some water, orange zest, orange juice and cinnamon and bake the plums for around 1.5-2 hours until thickened, if not continue baking. The jam should be gelled enough to spoon it into the jars.

2. Spoon the freshly baked jam into the sterilized jars up to 1/5 inch from the top and seal the jars.

3. Flip the jars upside down or boil for around 10 minutes and then leave to cool. Check the lids by pressing them with the finger. In case some of the jars with the orange and plum jam are unsealed, place them into the fridge or reprocess the unsealed jars.

Nutritional Information (1 tbsp):

Calories: 58; Total fat: 4 oz; Total carbohydrates: 11 oz; Protein: 3 oz

Orange Plum Jam

Prep Time: 40 min. | Makes: 6-7 11 oz jars

Ingredients:

5 lb plums, pitted and halved

2 oranges, cubed

1 tbsp. orange zest, minced

4 cups of sugar

2 tbsp. orange juice

1 tsp. cinnamon

How to Prepare:

1. Boil the plums and oranges with the sugar over medium heat for around 40 minutes, stirring all the time until thickened. Remove the foam from the surface.

2. Spoon some jam on a plate and wait until thickened, if not continue boiling and testing. The jam should be thick enough to spoon it into the jars. Few minutes before the jam is ready stir in the orange zest, orange juice, and cinnamon.

3. When the jam is ready, remove the saucepan from the heat and ladle freshly cooked plum jam into sterilized jars up to 1/5 inch from the top and seal the jars.

4. Flip the jars with the plum jam upside down or boil for around 10 minutes and then leave to cool.

Nutritional Information (1 tbsp):

Calories: 59; Total fat: 10 oz; Total carbohydrates: 8 oz; Protein: 2 oz

Baked Apple Jam

Prep Time: 50 min. | Makes: 6-7 11 oz jars

Ingredients:

5 lb sweet Gala or Fuji apples, peeled and cubed

4 cups of sugar

2 tbsp. citric acid

1 tbsp. cinnamon

How to Prepare:

1. Preheat the oven to 300°-350° Fahrenheit, combine the apples with the sugar and mix in the citric acid and cinnamon to bake the apples for around 50 minutes until thickened, if not continue baking.
2. Spoon the freshly baked jam into the sterilized jars up to 1/5 inch from the top and seal the jars.
3. Flip the jars upside down or boil for around 10 minutes and then leave to cool.

Nutritional Information (1 tbsp):

Calories: 59; Total fat: 4 oz; Total carbohydrates: 10 oz; Protein: 3 oz

Vanilla Raspberry Jelly

Prep Time: 1 hour | Makes: 8 10 oz jars

Ingredients:

3 lbs raspberries

5 cups of sugar

2 tsp. citric acid

3 tsp. pure vanilla extract

How to Prepare:

1. Spoon 1 cup of the sugar over the berries. Set aside for overnight.
2. Boil the raspberries over the low heat for around 30 minutes, stirring all the time. Pour in some water. Then mash the berries using the potato masher and strain the mixture to get 4-5 cups of the juice.
3. In a saucepan, combine the juice with the remaining sugar and boil the juice for 30 minutes until thickened. The jelly should be thick enough to pour it into the jars. Skim the foam from the surface. 10 minutes before the jelly is ready mix in the citric acid and pure vanilla extract.
4. Remove the saucepan from the heat and pour the freshly cooked jelly into the sterilized jars.
5. Turn the jars upside down or boil for around 10 minutes and then leave to cool. Check the lids by pressing them with the finger. In case some of the jars with the jelly are unsealed, place them into the fridge or reprocess the unsealed jars.

Nutritional Information (1 tbsp):

Calories: 58; Total fat: 6 oz; Total carbohydrates: 10 oz; Protein: 4 oz

Peach Jam

Prep Time: 30 min. | Makes: 4-5 11 oz jars

Ingredients:

3 lb peaches, peeled and cubed

5 cups of sugar

2 tbsp. lime juice

How to Prepare:

1. Boil the peaches with the sugar over low heat for around 30 minutes, stirring all the time until the sugar dissolves. Remove the scum from the surface.

2. Pour some jam on a plate and check if it has gelled enough, by pressing with the finger, if not continue boiling and testing. The jam should be thick enough to spoon it into the jars. Few minutes before the jam is ready stir in the lime juice.

3. When the jam is ready, remove the saucepan from the heat and ladle freshly cooked jam into the sterilized jars up to 1/5 inch from the top and seal the jars.

4. Seal the jars and then process them in a water bath. In a large pot, boil the jars for around 10 minutes and then take them out and leave to cool. Check the lids by pressing them with the finger. In case some of the jars with the peach jam are unsealed, place them into the fridge or reprocess the unsealed jars.

Nutritional Information (1 tbsp):

Calories: 55; Total fat: 2 oz; Total carbohydrates: 7 oz; Protein: 1.8 oz

Pineapple Taste Cherry Jelly

Prep Time: 1 hour | Makes: 6-7 11 oz jars

Ingredients:

2 lbs cherries, pitted

2 tbsp. pure pineapple extract

5 cups of sugar

2 tsp. citric acid

How to Prepare:

1. Spoon 1 cup of sugar over the berries and set aside for overnight.
2. Boil the berries over the low heat for around 30 minutes, stirring all the time. Then add in the pure pineapple extract and mash the berries with the potato masher. Strain the mixture to get 5 cups of the juice.
3. In a saucepan, combine the juice with the remaining sugar and boil the juice for around 30 minutes until thickened. The jelly should be thick enough to pour it into the jars. Skim the foam from the surface. 10 minutes before the jelly is ready mix in the citric acid.
4. Remove the saucepan from the heat and pour the freshly cooked jelly into the sterilized jars.
5. Turn the jars upside down or boil for around 10 minutes and then leave to cool. Check the lids by pressing them with the finger. In case some of the jars with the cherry jelly are unsealed, place them into the fridge or reprocess the unsealed jars.

Nutritional Information (1 tbsp):

Calories: 57; Total fat: 4 oz; Total carbohydrates: 8 oz; Protein: 3 oz

Apricot Jam

Prep Time: 35 min. | Makes around 5 11 oz jars

Ingredients:

3 lb small apricots, cubed

4 cups of sugar

2 tsp. citric acid

How to Prepare:

1. Wash and cube the apricots and place them into a big saucepan and then spoon the sugar over the apricots. Crack few stones and place the apricot kernels into the saucepan, this step will add specific flavors and an unforgettable taste to your apricot jam.

2. Boil the apricots over low heat for around 25-35 minutes, stirring all the time.

3. Mix in the citric acid and keep stirring until the apricots mixture has gelled. Put some jam on the plate and press down with your finger to check the density. Continue boiling and testing every five minutes until thickened.

4. Remove the saucepan with the apricot jam from the heat and carefully pour freshly cooked jam into the hot and sterilized jars up to 1/5 inch from the top.

5. Seal the jars and then turn them upside down or boil for around 10 minutes and then leave to cool. Check the lids by pressing them with the finger. In case some of the jars with the apricot jam are unsealed, place them into the fridge or reprocess the unsealed jars.

Nutritional Information (1 tbsp):

Calories: 62; Total fat: 0 oz; Total carbohydrates: 0.9 oz; Protein: 0.3 oz

Vanilla Apricot Jam

Prep Time: 35 min. | Makes around 5 11 oz jars

Ingredients:

6 cups of apricots, chopped

4 cups of sugar

2 tsp. lemon juice

2 tsp. vanilla

How to Prepare:

1. Wash and chop the apricots and place them into the pot and then mix in the sugar. Leave the apricots for at least few hours unrefrigerated at room temperature.

2. Boil the apricots over medium heat for around 30 minutes, stirring all the time until the sugar dissolves. Remember to remove the scum from the surface.

3. Mix in the lemon juice and vanilla and keep stirring until the apricots mixture has gelled. Put some apricot jam on the plate and press down with your finger to check the density. Continue boiling and testing every five or ten minutes until thickened enough to spoon it into the jars.

4. Remove the pot with the apricot jam from the heat and carefully spoon freshly cooked jam into the hot and sterilized jars up to 1/5 inch from the top.

5. Seal the jars and then turn them upside down or boil for around 10 minutes and then leave to cool. Check the lids by pressing them with the finger. In case some of the jars with the apricot jam are unsealed, place them into the fridge or reprocess the unsealed jars.

Nutritional Information (1 tbsp):

Calories: 60; Total fat: 0 oz; Total carbohydrates: 0.7 oz; Protein: 0.2 oz

Sugar-Free Apricot Jam

Prep Time: 40 min. | Makes around 5 10 oz jars

Ingredients:

3 lb apricots, cubed

3 tbsp. erythritol

20 drops of stevia

4 tbsp. honey

2 tsp. citric acid

How to Prepare:

1. Wash and cube the apricots and place them into a big saucepan and then spoon the honey over the apricots. Crack few apricot stones and place the apricot kernels into the saucepan, this step will add specific flavors and an unforgettable taste to your apricot jam.

2. Boil the apricots over medium heat for around 40 minutes, stirring all the time. Remember to remove the foam from the surface.

3. Mix in the erythritol, stevia and citric acid and keep stirring until the apricots mixture has gelled. Put some jam on the plate and press down with your finger to check the density. Continue boiling and testing every five minutes until thickened.

4. Remove the saucepan with the sugar-free apricot jam from the heat and carefully pour freshly cooked jam into the hot and sterilized jars up to 1/4 inch from the top.

5. Seal the jars and then turn them upside down or boil for around 10 minutes and then leave to cool. Check the lids by pressing them with the finger. In case some of the jars with the apricot jam are unsealed, place them into the fridge or reprocess the unsealed jars.

Nutritional Information (1 tbsp):

Calories: 48; Total fat: 0 oz; Total carbohydrates: 4 oz; Protein: 1 oz

Orange Apricot Jelly

Prep Time: 50 min. | Makes around 5 10 oz jars

Ingredients:

3 lb apricots, cubed

4 cups of sugar

2 cups of orange juice

2 tbsp. orange zest, minced

2 tsp. citric acid

How to Prepare:

1. Place the apricots into a big saucepan and then boil them with the water for around 15-20 minutes. Then strain the apricots to get 4-5 cups of the juice.

2. In a saucepan, combine the apricot juice with the sugar, orange juice, orange zest, and citric acid and boil the juice for 30 minutes until the sugar dissolves. Remove the foam from the surface. Pour some jelly on the plate to check the density. Continue boiling and testing every five minutes until thickened.

3. Remove the saucepan from the heat and ladle the freshly cooked jelly into the sterilized jars and seal the jars.

4. Flip the jars upside down or boil for around 10 minutes and then leave to cool. In case some of the jars with the orange apricot jelly are unsealed, place them into the fridge or reprocess the unsealed jars.

Nutritional Information (1 tbsp):
Calories: 49; Total fat: 4 oz; Total carbohydrates: 8 oz; Protein: 2 oz

Apple Pumpkin Jam

Prep Time: 50 min. | Makes around 8 11 oz jars

Ingredients:

3 lb pumpkin, peeled and cubed

2 apples, peeled and sliced

4 cups of sugar

half cup of apple juice

How to Prepare:

1. Place the pumpkin and apples into a big saucepan and spoon the sugar on top and leave for at least few hours unrefrigerated at room temperature or place in the fridge overnight.

2. In a saucepan, combine the pumpkin, apples, and apple juice and simmer the pumpkin mixture for 40 minutes until the sugar dissolves and pumpkin is soft. Remember to skim the foam from the surface. The apple pumpkin jam should be gelled enough to ladle it into the jars.

3. Ladle the freshly cooked apple pumpkin jam into the sterilized and hot jars and seal the jars.

4. Flip the jars upside down or boil for around 10 minutes and then leave to cool. In case some of the jars with the apple pumpkin jam are unsealed, place them into the fridge or reprocess the unsealed jars.

Nutritional Information (1 tbsp):
Calories: 55; Total fat: 0 oz; Total carbohydrates: 0.8 oz; Protein: 0 oz

Orange Gooseberry Jam

Prep Time: 40 min. | *Makes around 6 11 oz jars*

Ingredients:

5 lb gooseberries

2 oranges, sliced

2 tbsp. orange zest, minced

5 cups of sugar

3 tbsp. orange juice

How to Prepare:

1. In a saucepan, combine the gooseberries and oranges with the sugar and leave for few hours unrefrigerated at room temperature. Then boil the gooseberries and oranges with the sugar for 40 minutes, stirring until the sugar dissolves. Skim the foam and scum from the surface.

2. Five minutes before the jam is ready mix in the orange juice and orange zest and keep stirring until the orange gooseberry jam has gelled.

3. Ladle freshly cooked orange gooseberry jam into hot and sterilized jars up to 1/5 inch from the top and then seal the jars.

4. Flip the jars with the orange gooseberry jam upside down or boil for around 10 minutes and then leave to cool. Check the lids by pressing them with the finger. In case some of the jars

with the orange gooseberry jam are unsealed, place them into the fridge or reprocess the unsealed jars.

Nutritional Information (1 tbsp):

Calories: 48; Total fat: 0 oz; Total carbohydrates: 1 oz; Protein: 0 oz

Cherry Peach Jam

Prep Time: 40 min. | Makes around 6 11 oz jars

Ingredients:

4 cups cherries, washed and stoned

2 lb peaches, washed and sliced

5 cups of sugar

2 tbsp. lemon juice or 2 tsp. citric acid

How to Prepare:

1. In a big pot, combine the sliced peaches with the cherries and add the sugar on top. Leave for few hours unrefrigerated at room temperature.

2. Boil the fruits with the sugar for 40 minutes, stirring until the sugar dissolves. Remove the foam from the jam surface.

3. Few minutes before the jam is ready mix in the lemon juice or citric acid and keep stirring until the jam has gelled.

4. Spoon the freshly cooked cherry peach jam into the sterilized jars up to 1/5 inch from the top and then seal the jars.

5. Now turn the jars upside down and leave them for at least ten hours or for overnight to cool completely and only then turn them back. Check the lids by pressing them with the finger. In case some of the jars with the cherry peach jam are unsealed, place them into the fridge or reprocess the unsealed jars.

Nutritional Information (1 tbsp):
Calories: 67; Total fat: 0.4 oz; Total carbohydrates: 2 oz; Protein: 0 oz

Lemon Apricot Jam

Prep Time: 40 min. | Makes around 6 11 oz jars

Ingredients:

4 lb apricots, washed and sliced

3 tbsp. lemon zest, minced

5 cups of sugar

4 tbsp. lemon juice

How to Prepare:

1. In a large saucepan, combine the apricots and sugar and boil over medium heat for around 40 minutes, stirring all the

time with a spoon until the sugar dissolves. Take a big spoon and remove the scum from the surface.

2. Spoon some jam on a plate and wait until gelled, if not continue boiling and testing. The jam should be thick enough to spoon it into the jars.

3. Few minutes before the jam is ready mix in the lemon juice and lemon zest and keep stirring until the apricot mixture has thickened.

4. When the lemon apricot jam is ready, remove the saucepan from the heat and spoon freshly cooked jam into sterilized jars up to 1/5 inch from the top.

5. Seal the jars with the lemon apricot jam and flip them upside down or boil for around 10 minutes and then leave to cool. Check the lids by pressing them with the finger. In case some of the jars with the lemon apricot jam are unsealed, place them into the fridge or reprocess the unsealed jars.

Nutritional Information (1 tbsp):

Calories: 64; Total fat: 0.2 oz; Total carbohydrates: 1.6 oz; Protein: 0 oz

Vanilla Blueberry Jam

Prep Time: 40 min. | Makes around 6 10 oz jars

Ingredients:

5 cups of blueberries, fresh

5 cups of sugar

3 tsp. vanilla

How to Prepare:

1. In a big pot, combine the blueberries, sugar, and vanilla and boil over medium heat for around 40 minutes, stirring all the time until the sugar dissolves. Remove the foam and the scum from the vanilla blueberry jam.

2. Spoon some vanilla blueberry jam on a plate and wait until gelled. Check by pressing with the finger or the spoon, if not gelled enough continue boiling and testing every 5-10 minutes until gelled.

3. When the vanilla blueberry jam is ready, remove the pot with the blueberries from the heat and pour freshly cooked jam into sterilized and hot jars up to 1/4 inch from the top.

4. Seal the jars with the vanilla blueberry jam and flip them upside down or boil them for around 10 minutes and then leave to cool. Check the lids by pressing them with the finger. In case some of the jars with the vanilla blueberry jam are unsealed, place them into the fridge or reprocess the unsealed jars.

Nutritional Information (1 tbsp):
Calories: 59; Total fat: 3 oz; Total carbohydrates: 4 oz; Protein: 2 oz

Vanilla Plum Jam

Prep Time: 40 min. | Makes around 6 11 oz jars

Ingredients:

5 lb plums, stoned

4 cups of sugar

1 tsp. citric acid

2 tsp. vanilla

How to Prepare:

1. Halve the plums and boil them with the sugar over medium heat for 40 minutes, stirring all the time and removing the foam from the surface.

2. Spoon some jam on a plate and wait until gelled, if not continue boiling and testing every few minutes. The vanilla

plum jam should be thick and gelled enough to spoon it into the jars. Five minutes before the jam is ready mix in the citric acid and vanilla.

3. Remove the saucepan from the heat and spoon the freshly cooked jam into the sterilized jars up to 1/4 inch from the top and seal the jars.

4. Flip the jars with the vanilla plum jam upside down or boil them for around 10 minutes and then leave to cool. Check the lids by pressing them with the finger. In case some of the jars with the vanilla plum jam are unsealed, place them into the fridge or reprocess the unsealed jars.

Nutritional Information (1 tbsp):

Calories: 52; Total fat: 0 oz; Total carbohydrates: 0 oz; Protein: 0 oz

Baked Vanilla Plum Jam

Prep Time: 2 hours | Makes around 7 11 oz jars

Ingredients:

6 lb plums, stoned and halved

one cup of water

5 cups of sugar

3 tsp. vanilla

baking spray or unsalted butter

How to Prepare:

1. Combine the stoned and halved plums with the sugar and preheat the oven to 300°-360° Fahrenheit and then coat the baking pan with the baking spray or unsalted butter.

2. Pour one cup of water and mix in three teaspoons vanilla and bake the plums for around 1.5-2 hours until thickened and gelled enough to spoon the plum jam into the jars. If the vanilla plum jam is not gelled enough continue baking and testing every five or ten minutes. The plum jam should be gelled enough to spoon it into the jars.

3. Spoon the freshly baked vanilla plum jam into the sterilized and hot jars up to 1/5 inch from the top and seal the jars.

4. Flip the jars upside down or boil for around 10 minutes and then leave to cool. Check the lids by pressing them with the finger. In case some of the jars with the vanilla and plum jam

are unsealed, place them into the fridge or reprocess the unsealed jars.

Nutritional Information (1 tbsp):

Calories: 58; Total fat: 7 oz; Total carbohydrates: 8 oz; Protein: 3 oz

Baked Pear Jam

Prep Time: 50 min. | Makes around 7 11 oz jars

Ingredients:

5 lb sweet pears, peeled and cubed

4 cups of sugar

5 tbsp. lemon juice

1 tbsp. cinnamon

baking spray or butter

How to Prepare:

1. Wash and peel the pears and then cube them. Spoon the sugar and pour the lemon juice over the pears and set aside for around 2 to 3 hours unrefrigerated at room temperature.

2. Preheat the oven to 300°-350° Fahrenheit and then coat the baking pan with the baking spray or butter.

3. Spoon the cinnamon over the pears. Then bake the pears with the sugar, lemon juice, and cinnamon for around 40 minutes until thickened and gelled enough, if not continue baking and testing every five to ten minutes. The pear jam should be gelled enough to ladle it into the jars.

4. When the pear jam is ready ladle the freshly baked jam into the sterilized and hot jars up to 1/4 inch from the top and then seal the jars.

5. Flip the jars upside down or boil for around 10 minutes and then leave to cool. Check the lids by pressing them with the finger. In case some of the jars with the pear jam are unsealed, place them into the fridge or reprocess the unsealed jars.

Nutritional Information (1 tbsp):

Calories: 45; Total fat: 0 oz; Total carbohydrates: 0 oz; Protein: 0 oz

Vanilla Apple Jam

Prep Time: 40 min. | Makes around 5 10 oz jars

Ingredients:

10 big and sweet Fuji apples, peeled and cubed

5 cups of sugar

3 tsp. vanilla

2 tsp. citric acid

How to Prepare:

1. Wash and peel the Fuji apples and then cube them. Spoon the sugar and citric acid over the apples and set aside for around 1 to 2 hours unrefrigerated at room temperature or place in the fridge for overnight.

2. Boil the apples with the sugar over medium heat for around 40 minutes, stirring all the time.

3. Few minutes before the apple jam is ready mix in the vanilla. Remove the saucepan from the heat and ladle freshly cooked jam into sterilized jars up to 1/5 inch from the top.

4. Flip the jars with the vanilla apple jam upside down or boil for around 10 minutes and then leave to cool. Check the lids by pressing them with the finger. In case some of the jars with the vanilla apple jam are unsealed, place them into the fridge or reprocess the unsealed jars.

Nutritional Information (1 tbsp):

Calories: 46; Total fat: 4 oz; Total carbohydrates: 8 oz; Protein: 2 oz

Cherry Jelly with Raspberries and Oranges

Prep Time: 1 hour | Makes: 8 10 oz jars

Ingredients:

2 lbs cherries, pitted

2 lbs raspberries

4 oranges, peeled and diced

5 cups of sugar

2 tsp. citric acid

How to Prepare:

1. Spoon 1 cup of the sugar over the berries and oranges. Set aside for overnight.

2. Boil the berries and oranges over the low heat for around 30 minutes, stirring all the time. Pour in some water. Then mash the berries using the potato masher and strain the mixture to get 4-5 cups of the juice.

3. In a saucepan, combine the juice with the remaining sugar and boil the juice for 30 minutes until thickened. The jelly should be thick enough to pour it into the jars. Skim the foam from the surface. 10 minutes before the jelly is ready mix in the citric acid.

4. Remove the saucepan from the heat and pour the freshly cooked jelly into the sterilized jars.

5. Turn the jars upside down or boil for around 10 minutes and then leave to cool. Check the lids by pressing them with the finger. In case some of the jars with the jelly are unsealed, place them into the fridge or reprocess the unsealed jars.

Nutritional Information (1 tbsp):

Calories: 57; Total fat: 4 oz; Total carbohydrates: 8 oz; Protein: 3 oz

Blueberry Pears Jelly

Prep Time: 1 hour | Makes: 8 10 oz jars

Ingredients:

3 lb blueberries

1 lb pears, peeled and diced

5 cups of sugar

2 tsp. citric acid

How to Prepare:

1. Spoon 1 cup of the sugar over the berries and pears. Set aside for overnight.
2. Boil the blueberries and pears over the low heat for around 30 minutes, stirring all the time. Pour in some water. Then mash the blueberries and pears using the potato masher and strain the mixture to get 4-5 cups of the juice.
3. In a saucepan, combine the juice with the remaining sugar and boil the juice for 30 minutes until thickened. The jelly should be thick enough to pour it into the jars. Skim the foam from the surface. 10 minutes before the jelly is ready mix in the citric acid.
4. Remove the saucepan from the heat and pour the freshly cooked jelly into the sterilized jars.
5. Turn the jars upside down or boil for around 10 minutes and then leave to cool. Check the lids by pressing them with the finger. In case some of the jars with the jelly are unsealed, place them into the fridge or reprocess the unsealed jars.

Nutritional Information (1 tbsp):

Calories: 57; Total fat: 4 oz; Total carbohydrates: 8 oz; Protein: 3 oz

Mango-Raspberry Jam

Prep Time: 50 min. | Makes: 3-4 10 oz jars

Ingredients:

2 lb raspberries

3 medium mangos, peeled and diced

4 cups of sugar

5 tbsp. orange juice

How to Prepare:

1. Spoon the sugar over the raspberries and set aside for at least few hours.
2. Boil the raspberries with the sugar on a medium heat for 40 minutes, stirring all the time until thickened. Remove the scum from the surface. Few minutes before the jam is ready mix in the orange juice.
3. Pour the raspberry jam into the sterilized jars up to 1/4 inch from the top and seal the jars. Then flip the jars upside down or boil for around 10 minutes and then leave to cool. Check the lids by pressing them with the finger. In case some of the jars with the jam are unsealed, place them into the fridge or reprocess the unsealed jars.

Nutritional Information (1 tbsp):

Calories: 57; Total fat: 5 oz; Total carbohydrates: 9 oz; Protein: 4 oz

Blackberry Jelly

Prep Time: 1 hour | Makes: 8 10 oz jars

Ingredients:

3 lb blackberries

5 cups of sugar

3 tsp. citric acid

How to Prepare:

1. Spoon 1 cup of the sugar over the berries. Set aside for overnight.
2. Boil the blackberries on a low heat for around 30 minutes, stirring all the time. Pour in some water. Then mash the blackberries using the potato masher and strain the mixture to get 4-5 cups of the juice.
3. In a saucepan, combine the juice with the remaining sugar and boil the juice for 30 minutes until thickened. The jelly should be thick enough to pour it into the jars. Skim the foam from the surface. 10 minutes before the jelly is ready mix in the citric acid.
4. Remove the saucepan from the heat and pour the freshly cooked jelly into the sterilized jars or bottles.
5. Turn the jars upside down or boil for around 10 minutes and then leave to cool. Check the lids by pressing them with the finger. In case some of the jars or bottles with the blackberry jelly are unsealed, place them into the fridge or reprocess the unsealed jars.

Nutritional Information (1 tbsp):

Calories: 58; Total fat: 6 oz; Total carbohydrates: 10 oz; Protein: 4 oz

Conclusion

Thank you for buying this homemade jams and jellies cookbook. I hope this cookbook was able to help you to prepare delicious fruit jams or jellies recipes.

If you've enjoyed this book, I'd greatly appreciate if you could leave an honest review on Amazon.

Reviews are very important to us authors, and it only takes a minute for you to post.

Your direct feedback could be used to help other readers to discover the advantages of jams and jellies!

Thank you again and I hope you have enjoyed this cookbook.

Printed in Great Britain
by Amazon